Execution Day Journal

Written by:

Larry E. Peoples, Sr
Correctional Ofc. Lieutenant (Ret.)

(*Contains Mild Profanity*)

Chapter 1

It's 3:05 AM on a Friday morning and my alarm clock awakens me. I knock it off the side table trying to turn it off, as it breaks into three pieces. "Shit," I said as I try to be quiet and not wake up the whole house.

I quickly shower, shave and put on my T-Shirt, socks and underwear. I gulp down a piece of toast and jelly with some reheated coffee. "Blah," I say because this reheated coffee tastes like crap to me.

I put my chevrons and name-tag onto my long-sleeved uniform shirt and dress into my full uniform. I check on all of my children and wife before I leave our small, block house on "the circle" to work another execution.

I walk outside into the darkness and breathe in the air. It's cool and crisp this morning. I'm close enough to smell the New River. We live on state property only half a mile from the Florida State Prison.

I arrive at F.S.P. Main Unit and park in the back row of the parking lot. I look across to the road and see a few bright lights with people milling around. Some are carrying signs. Some are just sitting down praying. These are the anti-death penalty people. They hold a vigil for every execution. The pro-death penalty people rarely show up because they probably feel that what's going to happen is inevitable justice.

Locking my car, I enter the double doors of the Administration Building. I see many familiar faces. For this special duty, the Warden and the Central Office Staff like to keep the same small group. It's a matter of efficiency. For most of us, this is one of many executions we have participated in.

It's about 4:00 AM so I pick up two Styrofoam containers filled with breakfast and head to the main gate next to Tower #2. The officer up in the tower recognizes me and opens the gates. I enter the Auxiliary Control Room area where I'm admitted after I show my I.D.

I walk to the main Control Room and enter 'Times Square' through a pull gate. "Times Square" is so-called because it's where the corridors connect North to South and East to West.

The Sergeant on duty hands me a walkie-talkie and puts a heavy set of big, brass Folger Adam keys through the key portal. I go through another set of gates until I exit to the outside through the West Door.

I have to walk down a paved road inside the fence line to get to the back of the Death House. As I walk down the road I'm hit by bright spotlights from every angle. The Tower Officers are awake and alert at least. I wave and stop. I then realize the Control Room forgot to announce my presence in the yard. It's now 4:10 AM. "Stupid bastards," I say out loud to myself about the Control Room staff, as I freeze and wait for clearance to walk around to the back of Q-Wing.

When I arrive at the back of Q-Wing I find and insert the backdoor Death House key and slowly turn it. The door opens easily and I step inside. "Damn! I thought they cleaned this yesterday" I said, as I stepped into the dark hallway in front of the witness chamber. It had a damp, musty smell.

"Nothing like being in a dark death house at 4:15AM to get your blood pumping" I said quietly to myself. I laughingly wondered if the ghosts that are purported to haunt this place are here in the dark with me. No matter. Time to turn on the lights. I shine my little flashlight at the breaker box on the wall and turn on all of the lights, as the Death House comes to life.

Chapter 2

Now that the area has been 'awakened' so to speak, some explanation of terms describing the area is appropriate at this time I think.

The Death House is the overall term that means anything on the bottom floor of Q-Wing. That's where everything happens.

The Death Chamber is where the actual Electric Chair sits, bolted to the floor.

The Witness Chamber is the separate room directly in front of the Electric Chair that has thick glass so that the witnesses can see the execution.

The Executioner's Waiting Area is the small room where the Executioner sits before he goes into the electrical booth to turn (yes turn) the switch.

The Electrical Switch Booth is where the Executioner and a Maintenance Electrician sits during the execution to turn the switch and electrocute the condemned.

The Death Watch area is the cell area where the condemned man or woman is housed until the execution or a stay of execution is received.

The Hallway is the connecting concrete portal between the East Side of Q-Wing (where the Death Watch area and the Executioner's Waiting Room is located) and the West Side of Q-Wing (where the Death Chamber and the Witness Chamber is located). This hallway goes across the central plumbing pipe alley and concrete drainage channel, which is where water and toilet pipes are located for the 3-story Q-Wing. This hallway is also where they walk through with the inmate to sit them down in the chair.

There is also a room called the Electrical Vault, where a staff maintenance electrician is stationed during the execution to ensure enough amperage is available. This area is at the opposite end of the back entry to Q-Wing.

Also important to this story is the Bottom Floor Pipe Alley Door, which is located about 5 feet directly in front of the back door to Q-Wing. More about this door later.

Chapter 3

It's about 4:30 AM now, so I have a chance to sit down and take a rest before the Executioner is delivered. Of course, I choose to sit in the Electric Chair itself inside the Death Chamber. Creepy, I know, but the chairs in the Witness Chamber are hard, folding chairs and they hurt my tailbone and my back when I sit in them.

I glance forward and I see the reflection of myself sitting in the electric chair in the glass window separating the Witness Chamber and the Death Chamber. The last thing the condemned person sees, is themselves sitting in the Electric Chair. Think about that.

The writer and philosopher in me want to believe that it's Karma. That they too are now experiencing the mortal fear, terror and helplessness that their victim(s) felt.

But maybe not. G.O.K. (God Only Knows).

While I'm sitting there, I also flashback to a day about two years ago when I was chosen by the Colonel to play the condemned person during what is called a "Dry Run."

During a Dry Run, an Officer of approximately the same height, weight and gender is chosen to be strapped into the chair and have the procedure completed (without electricity, of course). This Dry Run is normally done on Day Shift, the day before a scheduled execution.

I reported to the Death Watch area where I was told to take off my shoes and socks and roll my left pants leg up above the knee. The Colonel and Assistant Warden got on my left and right sides. They each had a device called "The Claw." For those of you that are curious, internet savvy and want to see the devices, it was either the Argus Iron Claw or the Smith & Wesson Iron Claw. I'm not sure which.

These were two very old restraint devices that had two claw-like pincers that were placed onto the arm, right above the wrist. These pincers were then ratcheted down until the arm was restrained tightly. The shit hurt, that's all I know.

They both then grasped my hand with their free hand and bent my wrist back into a transport wrist-lock. The shit hurt even more! This got me up on my tip-toes, so I was going wherever the hell they wanted me to go at this point.

They both began to walk me through the Executioner's Waiting Area, in through the Hallway and around to the front of the Electric Chair where I was sat down very abruptly. Then another staff member buckled the chest strap and the arm straps. I was then released from the claws.

The waist strap was then buckled. Then the leg straps. The bottom, left leg strap had a metal electrode plate inside of it to attach the electrical wire.

Now comes the leather face mask and skull cap, with a screw attachment on top to connect the electric wire.

This is when the old leather smell hits you. You then realize that mostly dead people get to wear this. What could Rod Serling do with this mask? But I digress.

Now that you're all comfy in the chair, they do the proclamation rehearsal. They say something like 'having been found guilty of capital murder the sentence of death will now be carried out.' They ask you for any last words as the Warden holds up a microphone in front of you. I think I said something like "I should have pissed before I came down here," or something profound like that.

After the last statement, the chin strap is placed around your chin and then attached to the two wooden upright supports at head level on the back of the chair. The chin strap is tightened so much that no head or jaw movement is possible. You can still breathe, but if you are claustrophobic you're feeling it right now. But, I guess compared to what's about to happen to you, claustrophobia is down on the list of things to worry about.

A Maintenance Electrician wearing thick lineman gloves is standing behind you. He stays there behind the Chair during the execution to push down the skull cap if it should rise up and lose connectivity because of any movements the person makes during electrocution.

He reaches behind him on the wall to a wooden box (about the size of a foot locker) and attaches the electrical wires that come from inside the box. This is a transformer box.

One lead is bolted to the skull cap and the other lead is bolted to the leg. The electrician now pulls down a lever on the side of the box to connect the chair to the transformer, which is connected to the prison power plant outside the fence.

(As a side note, public utilities are not used to execute people in Florida. The entire prison is switched over to generator power. And NO. The lights don't dim either during an execution. That's Hollywood bullshit!)

While all this surreal stuff was happening to me, I spontaneously burst out laughing. I was thinking about the poor bastard they had do this once. He was a new guy who had been there about two weeks. He was on OJT (On Job Training). They had him strapped in and were at this point when the maintenance electrician purposely slammed down the heavy, wooden lid of the transformer not more than five feet behind the chair. It literally scared the living shit out of him. We had to send an empty transport van to the back door of Q-Wing to pick this guy up and take him home to change his drawers. He quit a month later.

Back to my story. They then lowered the leather hood that was attached to the facemask. More old leather smell. This covered my eyes. The purpose of this, of course, is to conceal the eyes from the witnesses. And again NO. The eyes don't pop out of the sockets or bleed profusely like you see in some movies. At least the executions I witnessed never did.

Then the Warden will nod to another Maintenance Electrician who is sitting next to the Executioner in the Electrical Switch Booth who both look through a small glass window at the Warden. The Maintenance Electrician turns a switch handle which then sends power to the switch handle of the Executioner. When the Warden nods again, the Executioner turns his handle. The electricity then flows through the person.

There is a cycle that the electrical equipment goes through to send enough amps through the person. Amperage kills the person, not volts. But the Warden has the option to allow the full cycle to continue or cut it short and turn off the "juice" to the person.

The only way I can describe it is, well…we've all seen one of those old-fashioned hot dog cookers where you stick a probe in both ends of the hot dog. The cord is plugged in and the hot dog cooks from the inside. That's what it looks like. Including the steam - or in this case…smoke.

Ooops. Back to the present. I see tail lights in the circle behind Q-Wing. The prison van is backing up to the back door of Q-Wing. Got to go open the door.

The Executioner cometh.

Chapter 4

It's about 4:45 AM and I go through the Witness Chamber to get to the back door of Q-Wing. A Lieutenant (who is in street clothes) slowly backs up a white, caged, prison transport van (used to securely transport inmates) toward the back door of Q-Wing.

I quickly open the back door of Q-Wing and swing it open enough so that I can close it against the side of the van. This prevents the Media across the street, who are in the open field, from seeing and photographing the Executioner going into the Death House.

The Lieutenant turns off the motor and locks the van. As he comes toward me I ask, "Have any
trouble L.T.?" "No. He was there. No delays." he said. "Good" I said. The L.T. puts the key into the back door of the van and unlocks the door. He then swings it open to reveal the Executioner sitting on one of the long bench seats inside the van.

The inside of the van is also painted white, so that the ambient light from inside the death house eerily illuminates the inside of the van. I look in and see a person wearing a long, black robe, with a black hood covering his face. His eyes are bloodshot red, but I can tell he is a white man. His skin is very light-colored around his eyes, which is all I can see of him because he has his hands inside the pockets of the robe.

Very unsettling. Very macabre. Although this isn't the first time I've seen this, the hair still stands up on the back of my neck.

This is death.

Chapter 5

As the executioner steps out of the van, he reaches his hand out to me to steady himself. I guess trying to climb out of a van and walk in that black robe and hood can be pretty difficult. His hand is cold and clammy. He smells of Lifebuoy and Scotch.

He grunts as his feet hit the ground. We all three walk into the Witness Chamber, through the Death Chamber, down the Hallway and finally into the Executioner's Waiting Room where he sits down on a leather couch.

He starts to remove his hood, and then his robe. "Too god damn hot in this thing" he says. I won't describe him other than to say he was an older man.

I hand him one of the breakfasts I have brought down. He opens the Styrofoam container and begins to eat it. Grits, eggs, toast, some patty sausage and a small container of milk. I turn on the oscillating fan and ask him if he needs anything else right now. He says "No thanks. I'm good."

It's about 4:55 AM as I walk over to the solid, steel door separating the Death Watch Cells and the Executioner's Waiting Room. I peel back the paper that has been taped onto the small glass window of the door. I see that the "Prep Team" is getting ready to shower and shave the condemned's head and leg up to above the knee. He should have had his last meal by now of whatever he wanted. Nothing over $100.00 worth of food usually.

I leave the Executioner and the L.T. alone for now and I return to the Death Chamber with my Styrofoam container. I decide against sitting in the Electric Chair to eat. It wouldn't look too good having spilled grits all over the arms.

I go to the Witness Chamber and pull open two of the hard chairs. One I sit on, one I eat on. While I'm eating I look through the Witness Chamber door and see the Bottom Floor Pipe Alley Door.

Memories begin to flow back.

Chapter 6

My mind flashes back to when I worked midnight shift on Q-Wing when I was a "new meat" officer. I was working with old "Pop" as everyone called him. Even the high ranking officers and administrators called him "Pop."

Pop showed me a lot about Q-Wing and how to do my job there. He showed me the right way to enter those cells in pitch black darkness and not get "shanked" (stabbed) while we fed breakfast. It seems Pop had some experience with getting shanked. Well at least one of his inmate runners (servers) did.

Pop told me he was feeding breakfast once with a new runner and he had an inmate on Q-2-East attach a shank to a broom handle. He stabbed the runner through the cell bars, right into his heart. He was pretty much D.R.T. (Dead Right There) in the cell area. Pop had to go in and pull the runner out from in front of the crazy bastards cell front.

Come to find out that the guy who was killed, wanted the guy who killed him to be his boy. A "Boy" in prison vernacular means a weak, turned-out sex partner. "Turned-out" means being anally raped in prison.

Pop also had stories about ghosts. Yes, the ghosts of Q-Wing. Pop would tell me that some nights he would leave the ventilation fans off to the Wing and keep the 2nd Floor pipe alley door open. The 2nd Floor was where the Officers Station was, so that's where we sat most of the night. Pop says it was so quiet sometimes he could hear sounds coming from the back of the Wing, on the bottom floor where the Death House is. He said it sounded like footsteps and voices. I never heard these noises. But who knows?

I was fascinated by what was downstairs in the Death House. At this point in my career, I hadn't been allowed inside the Death House. I had only heard about what was down there.

Once I remember I climbed down to the bottom floor of the pipe alley with the Wing keys and opened the Bottom Floor Pipe Alley Door and walked around. There was something about being down there in pitch darkness that didn't sit right with me. I felt like I was being watched.

Then all of a sudden I heard a loud voice. "Get your ass up here with those keys!" said Pop. He scared the hell out of me.

When I got back up to the 2nd floor, Pop was pissed. He said, "It's a good damn thing you didn't drop those keys into the water under the walkway. You would have been swimming in two feet of dirty water looking for them." "

Dumb-ass kid," said Pop.

Chapter 7

"Wake up, Sarge!" said the L.T. as he walked back through the

Witness Chamber out toward the transport van. "I'm awake, L.T. Just sitting here thinking about when I first started here at the F.S.P. Hilton" I said.

I got up from my empty breakfast styro and opened the back door of Q-Wing. He quickly got into the van and drove toward the sally port gate near Tower #7. His job was only halfway done for the day. He still had to come back in and pick up the Executioner and drop him off at the designated place after the execution.

Here's how it goes for him. At least this is how it used to go when Florida used the Electric Chair.

At a designated time and place, the L.T. drives a white, unmarked prison transport van to a pre-selected spot agreed upon by the Executioner and the Warden. The Executioner gets into the back of the van, where he is locked in by the L.T.

On the floor of the dark van is a hard plastic briefcase. Inside this briefcase is the black robe and black hood. The Executioner puts on the robe and hood and is taken to the prison. After the execution, the L.T. again picks up the Executioner in the unmarked van from the back of Q-Wing and transports him to the same spot or to another spot depending on the plan.

In the back of the van the Executioner has taken off the robe and hood. He opens the briefcase to find an envelope with $150 dollars in cash. He then takes the money for his services and replaces the robe and hood back into the briefcase.

When they reach the designated spot, the L.T. opens the back door of the van and the Executioner is left there. The L.T. then drives back to the prison.

The money is described in the official records (ironically) as used to pay an assistant electrician. No names are ever associated with this money.

Chapter 8

It's straight up 5:00 AM and things should begin to move along now. I turn on the window air conditioner in the witness chamber so it can cool the room and take out some of the musty smell.

I open and place 12 metal folding chairs along the window between the Witness Chamber and the Death Chamber. The Official State Witnesses are only about 5 feet away from the Electric Chair. Best seats in the house. Pun intended.

We used to have 12 small, specially-made wooden chairs for the official state witnesses to sit in. These chairs were made at the same time the original electric chair was built. They were probably made from the same wood, but they got old and started to crack and to break up.

I'm sure now they are souvenirs adorning the dens of many high-ranking officials within the Florida Department of Corrections.

Then I line up 12 more metal folding chairs for the media. We're expecting a big crowd in here this morning. A cop killer. So I had better put another 12 behind those for special witnesses of the Legislature, the Governors' Office, etc. You know…Bigwigs.

36 chairs later I'm done with the furniture arranging and set-up, so I walk back into the Executioners Waiting Room to check on him. He's doing a word search puzzle.

"Anything you need, sir?" I ask. "Everything is OK. But can you bring me some more milk?" he said. "I'll have the Prep Team get you some." I said.

I go over by the door to the Deathwatch Cell Area. I peel back the paper and knock on the little glass window in the door. One of the Prep Team turns around and walks toward the door. As he walks toward me, I can see that they already have the condemned man in a folding chair, cutting all his hair off.

He asks me what I needed. I told him that "The Man" wants some more milk. He nods his head and says he'll try to find some on one of the other wings upstairs. I nod too and tell the Executioner that they should be bringing him some more milk shortly.

I feel like I'm room service.

Chapter 9

Knocking on the back door to Q-Wing now is one of the Maintenance Electricians who wants to be let into the Electrical Vault to check something. He will be stationed in this area along with another Maintenance Electrician stationed behind the Electric Chair and another Maintenance Electrician sitting next to the executioner (as I explained earlier). Three electricians are needed to complete the impending task. It's now 5:25 AM.

At 5:30 AM the prison will switch over from the public electric company to generator power. The Maintenance Electrician jumps on to the extension phone inside the electrical vault and calls the Maintenance Superintendent. who is in the Main Control Room, to tell him everything is ready for the switch over.

The Main Control Room then notifies all the housing wings, medical clinic, all towers and kitchen by radio to tell them that the switch over is starting. This is done so these areas can be secured by lockdown when the lights go out for the minute or so it takes before the generator takes over.

I walk back quickly to tell the Executioner that the lights will be going off and on in a minute or so. I see that he got his milk. Ironically (I find out later), this was the milk the condemned inmate didn't open.

Dead man's milk. Yummy.

Chapter 10

Now at 5:32 AM the lights go out. I mean its dark. But it's a special kind of darkness inside of this prison. I guess because of the thick, concrete walls and because of what kind of things happen in here, it's like wearing a blanket of eerie darkness around you.

The lights going out now are a foreboding to all of the inmates.

The air is still and stale too, but it's not at all quiet. Inmates on other housing wings can be heard screaming about turning back on the lights all the way down here.

About two minutes later the lights go back on. The inmates keep screaming, with some of them banging their cell doors. Sounds like T-Wing is rockin-n-rollin. I wouldn't want to be on T-Wing right now. That place is the loudest wing in the building. Louder than any rock concert I've ever been to. The decibel level must be over 100 in there when they let loose.

Bang! Boom!! Ka-boom!!!

That is the sound of the large open population 'King Doors" slamming shut and being locked. That sound is an emergency signal to tell everyone that something is happening somewhere in the prison. You can hear it all over the building and outside too. I still hear that sound in my sleep to this day.

I learn from the radio broadcast over my walkie-talkie that an officer was assaulted on T-Wing. "Assholes!" I say out loud. "I hope they have to gas the piss out of them."

At 5:40 AM I return back to the Witness Chamber. As I walked past the Executioner lying on the couch, I see that he has fallen asleep. Too much Lifebuoy, I guess.

Within about 15 minutes, the situation on T-Wing has ended and the Control Room announces that we can resume normal operations. The Officer is OK, but the inmate who assaulted him is already having what is to become a very long, very bad day for him.

Karma. It's a bitch!

Chapter 11

It's now about 6:02 AM and my mind is wandering. The Colonel startles me as he approaches and says, "Sarge, everything going OK down here?" "Yes, Sir. Just like clockwork." I said.

Correctional Officer Chief is his official title, but he wears eagle insignias on his collar for the Colonel rank.

Colonel "T" is making his final inspection of the area before the execution. He checks the Electric Chair straps, the headpiece and the cleanliness of the Death Chamber. He checks out my set-up of the Witness Chamber and then walks around to the Electrical Vault to speak to the Maintenance Electrician.

As he walks back through to go upstairs, he says to me, "Sarge, go wake up the Executioner. He was snoring and drooling on himself when I first walked in. "Yes, Sir," I said. "I was just going back there."

I walk behind the Colonel into the Executioner's Waiting Area to see that the Executioner has awakened by himself. Colonel "T" nods his head and says good morning to him. The Executioner says good morning back and then adds curtly, "I hope I don't have to wait too long afterward. I'd like to get some fishing in this morning." The Colonel shrugs his shoulders and holds both palms upward. This is the international signal for "I don't know."

The Executioner then loudly burps and goes back to his word search puzzle. Colonel "T" then looks back at me. He sighs and shakes his head from side to side.

This is the international signal for "dumb-ass."

Chapter 12

It's about 6:30 AM now and the Executioner is back into his robe and hood, and is moved from his waiting area to the Electrical Switch Booth inside of the Death Chamber.

He and a Maintenance Electrician will sit there side-by-side until after the execution is over and all of the witnesses have left the building.

Inside of this booth are the switches. One handle the electrician turns first. The other one the executioner turns to send current to the condemned. There is no pull-down switch like in the movies here. Just two metal handles that are turned to the right and left.

The Warden steps into the Death Chamber to check on everything. He pulls back the curtain across the opening of the electrical booth and greets the Maintenance Electrician and Executioner with the same, "Hello." They both return his greeting.

Now a Sergeant is placed into the Death Chamber on the direct line phone to the Capital. He will stay on this phone until after the execution. He will be talking to someone in the Governor's Office to receive official word that there has been a stay of execution granted or that there has not been a stay of execution granted.

Legally, the execution is not supposed to begin before 7:00 AM. Now begins for me the seemingly long wait before the witnesses arrive.

Now begins for Jesse Tafero this very short time to live.

Chapter 13

Jesse Joseph Tafero (born October 12, 1946), was convicted for the murders of Florida Highway Patrol Officer Phillip Black and Donald Irwin, a visiting Canadian Constable and friend of Black.

Early on the morning of February 20, 1976, Trooper Black and Constable Irwin, approached a car parked at a rest stop for a routine check.

Jesse Tafero, Sonia Jacobs, two children, and Walter Rhodes, a prison friend of Tafero's were asleep in the car. While checking on the occupants, Trooper Black saw a gun on the floor of the car. He then woke everyone.

Trooper Black had Rhodes and then Tafero get out of the car. At some point after that, both the Trooper and the Constable were shot and killed.
After fleeing the scene in the Trooper's car they then dumped the patrol car. They kidnapped a man and stole his car. The three were later caught at a roadblock.

Tafero, Jacobs and Rhodes were all arrested. Rhodes turned state's evidence in exchange for a plea to a lesser charge. Tafero and Jacobs were tried and convicted of capital murder and sentenced to death.

Walter Rhodes confessed to shooting the officers after Tafero's execution and is still serving a Life Sentence in a Florida prison.

Years later, Sonia "Sunny" Jacobs conviction was overturned on appeal and she was released from prison.

Chapter 14

I hear the sound of engines approaching. I peek through the Venetian blinds in one of the windows of the Death Chamber. It's 6:43 AM. Yep. Two white, Dodge 15-passenger vans approaching from the sally port gate. It's show time!

I go to the back door of the Death House and swing open the heavy steel door. The first van arrives and stops. The doors are opened and the 12 official state witnesses climb out and head toward me. I motion them in and point to the door of the Witness Chamber.

Before now I have already locked the door to the Death Chamber so that the area is separated and secured.

The witnesses file in through both doors very quietly. I look at their faces and nod my head at all that look at me. Some just stare down at the ground as they walk in. A very somber group this morning.

Next come the media witnesses. I again point to the door of the Witness Chamber. They file in carrying their brand new pencils and blank steno pads. This is all that they are allowed to have. No cameras, no tape recorders. Just the basics. Most of these media people I've seen before on other executions.

A lady from within the media group almost falls off her high heels as she steps into the back door. She catches her nylon stocking on the rough, metal hinge of the back door. "Shit" she quietly says. I ask her if she is hurt, but she ignores me and continues on into the Witness Chamber. The 12 state witnesses always sit in the first row of chairs. Everyone else sits behind them.

Along with all of the witnesses from the vans, come a Medical Tech and a Registered Nurse with stethoscope and smelling salts. Just in case someone in the Witness Chamber faints or is taken ill.

It's only a matter of minutes now.

Chapter 15

It's quiet inside the Witness Chamber now as everyone is just waiting and watching. I secure the outside door and also the Witness Chamber door. I can hear the scratching of pencils from the media as some of them sketch the area, and some write down their thoughts. The van drivers are also inside the Witness Chamber to provide security.

It's packed tight in here. The air smells like a combination of women's perfume and musty air smell. I think to myself that they forgot to replace the air conditioner filter for the window unit when this room was cleaned down here.

Suddenly the rear door to the Death Chamber swings open. The Warden is first, closely followed by the Colonel, Tafero and the Assistant Warden.

The Colonel and the Assistant Warden walk Tafero around to the front of the Electric Chair and sit him down. While Tafero is still being held by the claws, the Warden and the Maintenance Electrician buckle the chest strap, the arm straps, the waist strap and the strap near the hands. Once these are tightened, the Colonel and Assistant Warden release their grips on Tafero.

Now comes the leg straps. The Colonel and Assistant Warden then buckle the leg straps. Colonel "T" makes sure that the leg electrode is securely attached to the leg.

Everyone in the room is fixated on this process. They are looking with horror and wonder at the same time. It is a well-choreographed process that it practiced, and then practiced again.

Once they have buckled all of the torso straps, Colonel "T" begins to check them again.

I'm now looking at Tafero too. He is looking down at the straps as they tighten and re-tighten them. His head is clean-shaven. He looks like a cue ball with a face.

As I'm watching this, Tafero finally looks up from the straps and into the Witness Chamber. He scans left to right. Then he looks right at me, smiles and nods. I can read these words from his lips. "Mister Peoples."

I coolly nod back, but inside I'm feeling disturbed.

Chapter 16

During my then nearly 9 years at Florida State Prison, I worked off and on with the Death Row inmates of S-wing and R-wing. As Officers, we grade inmates by how much of a pain in the ass they are. Jesse Tafero was never any problem to the Officers that I can recall. He always spoke respectfully to the Correctional Staff.

I can only recall once when he was written a D.R. (Disciplinary Report) for something. It was about a medical issue he was having. I think he very loudly called the Prison Doctor a "correspondence course" doctor. He kept loudly repeating this all the way out the door of the Medical Clinic. The Doctor got mad and had the Clinic Security Officer write him up for causing a disturbance.

Big deal. The guy was a shitty Doctor.

I remember that Tafero had his Death warrant signed in 1984 and I was one of his Death Watch Officers (Cell Front Monitor). My job was to write down everything he did inside of a Long Day Book. I would sit directly in front of his cell and note the time and description of anything that occurred. If Tafero went to the Medical Clinic, to the Non-Contact Visiting Park or anywhere else, I would come with him and bring my log book.

He talked about many things during this time. Life, love, children and regrets. The only thing we never talked about was the crime or the case in the courts. This was not allowed.

I believe that this time was when we became not friends, but were able to relate to one another as human beings.

Now it's time to watch him die.

Chapter 17

The Warden asks Tafero if he has a last statement. To this day, I can't recall if he said anything or not. I was so distracted by what had transpired before that I don't remember. I can recall in vivid detail just about everything else - except this. Strange.

The warden then asks the Sergeant on the phone in the Death Chamber if there is a stay of execution. The Sergeant shakes his head from side-to-side and says "No, Sir." He then hangs up the telephone. It's 7:06 AM.

The headpiece is now secured down on Tafero. The electrode

connection is checked by the Maintenance Electrician.

Now comes the chin strap. Tight, tighter, tighter.

Finally the leather hood is lowered over the eyes.

Just seconds to go.

The transformer box behind the chair is engaged.

The Warden looks in the direction of the Electrical Switch Booth.

He nods his head.

Chapter 18

I hear the switches engage. I begin to hear the whine from the transformer as the three cycles begin. Tafero stiffens up backwards as I hear the normal creaking sound of the wooden chair. I turn away from Tafero to look at the witnesses.

It is usually a very quiet process. But not this morning. I hear audible gasps from the people in the Witness Chamber.

Normally there is a small wisp of smoke coming from the head, and off of the leg that has the electrode attached. But not this time. I turn back to Tafero in time to see five to six inch mostly blue flames coming out from underneath the skull cap.

The only way to describe it is, it's like when you find your meat burning on the barbeque grill. You open the lid and the large flames come out from underneath.

This is what Tafero's head looked like. It appeared like we had caught the man on fire.

The Warden nodded at the Electrical Switch Booth. The electricity stopped. But Tafero looked like he was gasping for air. He did this about five times.

The Warden nodded at the Electrical Switch Booth again. The electricity was applied again. Tafero again stiffened and flames shot out from his head. This time he looked like he gasped for air while the electricity was still on. The Warden signaled to stop the electricity.

Billows of smoke had filled the Death Chamber by now. Some of the smoke went under the Witness Chamber door. The smell of human flesh was everywhere.

Once again the Warden nodded at the Electrical Switch Booth. The electricity was applied a third time. This time after a short time, the Warden audibly spoke to stop the electricity.

Tafero did not move except to slump back down in the chair. No flames. No breathing this time. Just smoke.

I could see through the smoke that the Warden looked livid.

Chapter 19

The Warden stood in front of Tafero and motioned the prison Medical Technician forward to assess him. The Med. Tech. pulled out his stethoscope and unbuttoned the middle two buttons of Tafero's dress shirt. He inserted the end and listened for what seemed like the longest minute in history. When he finished, he looked at the Doctor in the Death Chamber with him and nodded his head.

The prison Doctor then stepped forward, stethoscope and penlight in hand, and began to examine Tafero. After the Doctor had listened for the heartbeat (there was none) and raised the leather covering over the eyes and checked for pupil responsiveness (there was none) he looked at the Warden. "This man is deceased" said the Doctor.

This was my queue to head to the back door and open it. I could hear the Warden say on the microphone, "The sentence of the State of Florida versus Jesse Joseph Tafero has been carried out. Please exit to the rear."

So, with the normal sound of banging and scraping on the floor of the metal chairs, everyone filed out and headed back to the vans. Some witnesses looked fine. Some like the lady who tore her nylon stocking, looked like they were going to puke at any moment.

In my mind I was saying, "puke outside so I don't have to smell it." Ironic thought, I later determined, right after smelling burning human flesh.

When every one of the witnesses had left, I closed and locked the door. As I walked back into the Witness Chamber, I heard the Warden speaking to the remaining staff in the Death Chamber. "You all know that this is one deep, pile of shit we've just stepped into?" Everyone nodded. "Let's get the hell out of here and meet in my office in fifteen minutes," he said.

As I unlocked the connecting door between the Witness Chamber and the Death Chamber, the Warden looked at me and said, "Sarge, make sure the body is taken care of." "Yes, Sir" I said.

He and all of the other staff then walked out of the Death Chamber.

Then the Executioner and the Maintenance Electrician left the Electrical Switch Booth and headed back in the direction of the Executioner's Waiting Area.

Now it was just me and Tafero alone.

Chapter 20

I walked around to the front of the Electric Chair. By now the body had stopped smoking. I began to remove the headpiece. I took off the chin strap and the rest of the headpiece and placed it on one of the uprights of the back of the Electric Chair.

Tafero's head slumped forward and turned slightly to the right. I could see from this angle that a four inch diameter hole had been burned into the top of his skull. The fire had burned through all of the layers of skin. The fire had also cauterized the hole.

I unbuckled the leg electrode and the remaining straps, except for the chest strap, which I loosened to allow the body to slump forward. I walked around to the front of the Electric Chair and just looked.

Tafero had a look of anguish on his face. Not necessarily because he felt the pain of every amp surging through him, but most likely because he tensed up his face right before the electricity hit him. I don't think he felt a thing after the first cycle.

"Sarge, I'm here to help you with the body." I looked around and saw the Sergeant who had been on the telephone to the Capital entering the Death Chamber. "I've got most of it done" I said.

"I'll bet to the knee" he said. Unhesitatingly I said, "Not on this one, Sarge. Too much shit is coming down on us all after this one. Not today."

He was referring to a wager that was often made after an execution amongst the staff who remained in the Death Chamber to attend to the body.

When the body was leaned forward after loosening the chest strap, many times a thick drool began to come out of the mouth. People would shout out where the spit would break. The one who guessed right, got a quarter from all of the other participants.

Gallows humor, I guess. Witticism in the presence of death.

Chapter 21

By now the recently promoted Maintenance Superintendent had come down to retrieve the leg electrode and the headpiece with the sponge in it. He disconnected the electrical wires and placed both into a leather briefcase.

"The FDLE will be looking at those," I said under my breath. The Florida Department of Law Enforcement was the Statewide agency that would investigate this "clusterfuck."

It would later be revealed that the natural sea sponge normally soaked in saline water and used up inside of the headpiece for connectivity, was replaced by a synthetic, man-made sponge. So it was really the sponge that caught on fire, not Tafero.

But at this point in time it didn't matter to the media what it really was, it only mattered to them what it looked like.

Headlines would read "Tafero Execution Goes Horribly Wrong."

The media hates Correctional Officers and what we do anyways. They give us no respect. Living in a bubble like they do, with their heads up their collective asses makes agenda-driven "journalism" and the truth, sometimes mutually exclusive.

But it was still pretty funny that some of those media witnesses nearly puked.

Chapter 22

The Sallyport Gate Sergeant calls the phone in the Death Chamber to tell us that the hearse was coming in to pick up the body for the trip to Gainesville. The Medical Examiner must perform an autopsy on all executed inmates in Florida.

That goes back to the Spenkelink execution in May of 1979 when it was alleged that John Spenkelink was already dead when the electricity hit him. This was subsequently proven to be wrong. But after Spenkelink, a mandatory autopsy was performed.

Also with the Spenkelink execution came the change in procedure to walk the inmate into the Death Chamber and strap them in while being observed by all of the witnesses.

I wasn't there for that one, I was still in High School. But I understand that Spenkelink was already strapped into the chair, and then the blinds between the Death Chamber and the Witness Chamber were opened.

Not seeing Spenkelink walk in, lead to some ridiculous allegations from the media and some of their friends in the anti-death penalty crowd. Hence the change.

I open the back door of the Death House as the hearse slowly backs up to the door. I close the door against the side of the hearse to block the view of the media seeing us load the body.

Two guys get out and I recognize them from other executions. They recognize me too. We exchange greetings. These are the so-called "White Undertakers." Normally, the race of the deceased will determine who is called to pick up the body.

There are several reasons for this. Some State of Florida preferences. Some deceased inmates' family preferences. Some political preferences.

The back door of the hearse is opened up and a stretcher is pulled out and wheeled into the Death Chamber. I begin to unbuckle the chest strap as both attendants grab Tafero under the armpits. I grab both ankles and we lift Tafero out of the Electric Chair in unison.

We place the body on its back. The head is pushed down onto the stretcher. The legs are then pushed down and straightened out to lay flat on the stretcher. No leg bones have to be broken to get the body to lay flat. Just a firm push downward. Then the arms are folded over the chest and they are strapped down.

I place a shoebox of black dress shoes and white socks between the feet of Tafero. These will be placed on at the funeral home for the burial. Some have a funeral and burial, and some don't. Some are just cremated and given to the family.

The body is then covered by a velvet blanket with the name of the funeral home on it. The stretcher is then wheeled back out to the hearse and loaded. The two guys thank me, and I thank them in return. They then drive back toward the Sallyport gate to exit the prison.

They've told me before that they always purposely drive really slowly when they pass the media outside the prison for several reasons.

First, so photos and film can be taken by the media of the hearse with the body in the back.

Second, because the funeral director wants the name of his business, which is printed on the side of the hearse, splashed all over the world.

Third, because they want their friends and family to see them in the hearse.

For them, it's just cool being on TV.

Chapter 23

I leave the back door to the Death House open because I see that the white prison van is coming in through the Sallyport Gate and headed this way. I know what time it is.

I quickly go back to the Executioners Waiting Area and tell him to get ready to go. He puts his robe and hood back on and walks with me, stopping inside the Death Chamber next to the Electric Chair. He leans on one of the uprights waiting for the van to arrive.

"This was not good today" he says. "No, Sir" I said. "Not good at all." He looks down at the chair where Tafero was sitting a short time ago. He shakes his head and says, "I hope this doesn't put me out of a job."

I hear the van backing up to the door as I head out to close the door against the side of the van again. "Sir, we're ready for you" I said. He comes out through the Witness Chamber and toward the back door. He puts one foot on the van step to get in. He reaches out his hand and I grab it. His hand is still cold and clammy. I help him step up into the van.

When he is seated, I motion to the L.T. who exits the drivers' seat with the black briefcase in hand and gives it to the Executioner. The

L.T. closes and locks the van door and gets back into the van without saying a word.

He heads out of the Sallyport Gate and toward the back way between U.C.I. (Union Correctional Institution) and F.S.P. He'll cross a rickety wooden bridge over the New River and follow along their perimeter road until he reaches State Road 16. Then it's homeward bound for the Executioner.

Time for me to go home, too.

Chapter 24

By now it's after 8:00 AM.

I close and lock the door between the Witness Chamber and the Death Chamber. The metal chairs will be folded and stored by an inmate crew that comes in later in the day and cleans the area. I exit the back of Q-Wing and lock the metal door.

I begin my walk around back to the West Door. Luckily, when I get near the Sallyport Gate, I see a van coming in to pick up some supplies for the minimum security "O" Unit. I bum a ride to the West Door and enter the West Corridor. The prison has returned to normal operations by now.

I go through Times Square and dump my keys and walkie-talkie into the small access door of the Main Control Room. I exit Times Square and head for the Auxiliary Control Room again. I show my I.D. to the Officer and he let's me out of the two gates to the front door. I wave at the Tower #2 Officer and head for my car. Shortly I'm back on the Circle and at home.

Pulling up into my carport, I see my oldest girl with her head stuck out of the front door. "What the hell is she still doing here?" I quietly said out loud. She was supposed to be at school by now. I was so ready to go to sleep. "Pisses me off," I say under my breath.

I sigh and tell her to tell her Mother that I will be taking her to school now. She goes back inside, gets her book and tells her mother what I had said about taking her to school.

We drive and talk about why she is late. I'm just too tired to debate it.

I pull up, hug her and drop her off at Lake Butler Elementary School. If she only knew what was on that uniform.

I head toward the I.G.A. grocery store in town because I remember that I have to pick up candles, cake mix and frosting for a birthday party we are having tomorrow for my baby girl. She turned three yesterday. We decided to wait until Saturday to have the party so that more people could attend.

I find all of my items and exit the store. As I approach my car, I see someone waving to me at the other end of the parking lot, motioning me to come over.

It's the Executioner. He wants to talk.

Chapter 25

"I'm not supposed to talk to you! I'm not even supposed to be seen with you outside of the prison" I said very tersely and quietly to him. "I know" he said.

I looked around to see if any of the other staff who participated in this morning's execution were here. That's all I needed was to have one of them or a Prison Inspector see me with this guy.

He took a sip out of his can of Budweiser and got back into his pickup truck. The passenger side seat of the truck was littered with Coke and beer cans, and I could smell that this wasn't his first beer this morning.

"$150.00 dollars will buy a lot of beer" he said as he took another sip. I asked him what it was that he needed from me. "Information" he said. "I need to know if they're talking about shutting down the Electric Chair now." I shook my head and told him that I didn't know.

"Been doing this since Spenkelink. I got Bundy too" he said. " I got a lot more."

"I don't have a problem in the world killing those bastards" he said. "Mad dogs should be put down."

He continued. " I'll go home this morning and sleep like a baby. Don't bother me in the least." He was slurring his words, so I knew that he had imbibed on something stronger than beer already this morning.

"Sir, I've got to go home" I said. He then looked coldly at me, grabbed my arm and said, "Public service, that's what I do. A Public service."

And with that he turned the key in the ignition and drove off. I walked back to my car and sat there a minute before I headed home. To shower and to sleep.

He's a tortured soul too, I thought.

Another tortured soul.

Epilogue

The execution of Jesse Joseph Tafero occurred on May 4, 1990.

Execution procedures have changed these 24 years later, as the Electric Chair is no longer in general use. But the procedures I've written about in "Execution Day Journal" were accurate and did occur the way I described back in May of 1990.

I worked at the Florida State Prison near Starke, Florida from June of 1981 until I departed for Martin Correctional Institution near Indiantown, Florida in April of 1991.

This journal represents my recollection of events that I experienced and then subsequently documented almost 24 years ago, to serve as sort of a catharsis for me.

I worked many executions during my years there. My experiences inside FSP are numerous and truthful.

I was there. I saw this.

I did not fabricate this story nor piece it together from news accounts. This is NOT a work of fiction. My very detailed description about areas, procedures, people and events only come from first-hand experiences.

Larry E. Peoples, Sr.

Printed in Great Britain
by Amazon